3XKDR00006929-

W9-BKC-777

Follett
23.00

641.597 LOC

Locricchio, Matthew.

The cooking of Mexico

18,607

$22.00
23.00

DATE DUE	BORROWER'S NAME	ROOM NO.
10/31/03	Cindy Luna	4D
4/15	Carina Rostant	5Ch.

641.597 LOC

Locricchio, Matthew.

The cooking of Mexico

BROOKLYN AVE SCHOOL LIBRARY
VALLEY STREAM, NY 11581

796024 02280   02628C   006

THE COOKING OF
Mexico

Super Chef

MATTHEW LOCRICCHIO

WITH PHOTOS BY

JACK MCCONNELL

BENCHMARK BOOKS

MARSHALL CAVENDISH
NEW YORK

This book is dedicated to the people of Mexico.

ACKNOWLEDGMENTS

Cookbooks are the result of great teamwork and the cooperation of many people, and *The Cooking of Mexico* is certainly no exception. Many thanks go to the members of the Recipe Testers Club and their adult assistant chefs, whose testing, comments, and suggestions were invaluable. They are: Saun Ellis and Sonia Drohojowska of New Milford, Connecticut; Diane Carter, Molly Hall, and Sadie Hall of Santa Cruz, California; Virginia Locricchio Zerang and Nikolas Zerang of Glenview, Illinois; and Lisa Cooper-Weinberg and Joshua Weinberg of Prattsburg, New York. Also, special thanks to Francisco Drohojowski for his great help with my Spanish, Carlos Guiterez of the Mexican Cultural Institute for helping with my research, and John Strand for his recipe archives. Thanks also to Jack McConnell for his outstanding photographs, his assistant John Addario, and Marie Hirschfeld for her great food styling. My gratitude also goes to Paula McNamara; Southern Exposure of Mystic, Connecticut; Julie Allisi; and Raphaela LaMonica for their help.

Benchmark Books
Marshall Cavendish
99 White Plains Road
Tarrytown, New York 10591-9001
www.marshallcavendish.com
Text copyright © 2003 by Matthew Locricchio
Food photographs © 2003 Jack McConnell, McConnell, McNamara & Company
Art director for food photography: Matthew Locricchio
Map copyright © 2003 by Mike Reagan

Illustrations by Janet Hamlin
Illustrations copyright © 2003 by Marshall Cavendish Corporation

All rights reserved. No part of this book may be reproduced or utilized in any form or by any means electronic or mechanical including photocopying, recording, or by any information storage and retrieval system, without permission from the copyright holders.

Book design by Anahid Hamparian
Food styling by Marie Hirschfeld and Matthew Locricchio

Library of Congress Cataloging-in-Publication Data

Locricchio, Matthew.
  The cooking of Mexico / by Matthew Locricchio.
    p. cm.— (Superchef)
Includes index.
Summary: Introduces the different culinary regions of Mexico and presents many kinds of recipes for traditional Mexican dishes.
  ISBN 0-7614-1217-4
1. Cookery, Mexican—Juvenile literature.   [1. Cookery, Mexican.
  2. Food habits—Mexico.]   I. Title. II. Series.
  TX716.M4L544 2002
  641.5971—dc21
                                   2002002185
Photo Research by Rose Corbett Gordon, Mystic, CT
Photo Credits: p. 12: Robert Frerck/Stone/Getty Images; p. 14: Charles Sleicher/Stone/Getty Images; p. 16: Alison Wright/The Image Works

Printed in Italy
1   3   5   6   4   2

Contents

DEAR READER,

I WILL ALWAYS REMEMBER THE AROMA OF ONIONS, CELERY, AND BELL PEPPER COOKING IN MY MOTHER'S CAST-IRON DUTCH OVEN. THAT APPETIZING AROMA PERMEATES MY CHILDHOOD MEMORIES AS IT DID OUR HOME. ONE OF THE MOST DELIGHTFUL THINGS I HAVE LEARNED AS A CHEF IS HOW DEEPLY FOOD INFLUENCES OUR LIVES. FOOD TOUCHES PEOPLE ON SO MANY LEVELS—PHYSICALLY, EMOTIONALLY, SOCIALLY, AND SPIRITUALLY. THE PUBLIC'S INTEREST IN FOOD AND CUISINE IS INSATIABLE, AND I AM CONSTANTLY AMAZED AT THE LEVEL OF INTEREST AND KNOWLEDGE I SEE IN YOUNG PEOPLE. THE CUISINES OF THE WORLD ARE WIDE AND VARIED AND GIVE US A GOOD PICTURE OF HUMAN NATURE AT ITS BEST. A STUDY OF THE WORLD'S MANY DIFFERENT CUISINES UNVEILS THE RICH TAPESTRY OF CULTURAL DIFFERENCES, YET IN THE END WE LEARN ONE OF LIFE'S MOST VALUABLE LESSONS: FOOD BRINGS PEOPLE TOGETHER.

THESE COOKBOOKS, WHICH I HEARTILY ENDORSE, GIVE YOUNG PEOPLE THE CHANCE TO EXPLORE, TO CREATE, AND TO LEARN. IN **Superchef**, YOUNG READERS CAN USE THEIR HOME KITCHENS TO EXPLORE THE MANY DIFFERENT TASTES OF THE WORLD. THEY CAN LEARN THE VALUE OF WORKING TOGETHER WITH FAMILY MEMBERS IN THE HOME AND EXPERIENCE THE SHEER PLEASURE OF A PERFECT MEAL. WHEN THE CUTTING, CHOPPING, AND COOKING ARE OVER, IT'S TIME TO SIT DOWN TOGETHER AND ENJOY THE FRUITS OF THE ASPIRING CHEF'S LABOR. THIS IS WHEN YOUNG CHEFS CAN LEARN THE **REAL** SECRET OF THE GREAT CHEFS—THE JOY OF SHARING.

CHEF FRANK BRIGTSEN

Frank Brigtsen

BRIGTSEN'S RESTAURANT
NEW ORLEANS, LOUISIANA

From the Author

Welcome to **Superchef**. This series of cookbooks brings you traditional recipes from other countries, adapted to work in your kitchen. My goal is to introduce you to a world of exciting and satisfying recipes, along with the basic principles of kitchen safety, food handling, and common-sense nutrition. Inside you will find classic recipes from Mexico. The recipes are not necessarily all low-fat or low-calorie, but they are all healthful. Even if you are a vegetarian, you will find recipes without meat or with suggestions to make the dish meatless.

Many people today eat lots of fast food and processed or convenience foods because these are "quick and easy." As a result there are many people both young and old who simply don't know how to cook and have never experienced the pleasure of preparing a successful meal. **Superchef** can change the way you feel about cooking. You can learn to make authentic and delicious dishes from recipes that have been tested by young cooks in kitchens like yours. The recipes range from very basic to challenging. The instructions take you through the preparation of each dish step-by-step. Once you learn the basic techniques of the recipes, you will understand the principles of cooking fresh food successfully.

There is no better way to get to know people than to share a meal with them. Today, more than ever, it is essential to understand the many cultures that inhabit our planet. One way to really learn about a country is to know how its food tastes. You'll also be discovering the people of other countries while learning to prepare their classic recipes.

Learning to cook takes practice, patience, and common sense, but it's not nuclear science. Cooking certainly has its rewards. Just the simple act of preparing food can lift your spirits. Nothing brings family and friends together better than cooking and then sharing the meal you made. It can be fun, and you get to eat your mistakes. It can even lead to a high-paying career. Most importantly, you can be proud to say, "Oh, glad you liked it. I did it myself."

See you in the kitchen!

Matthew Locricchio

Before You Begin

A WORD ABOUT SAFETY

Safety and common sense are the two most important ingredients in any recipe. Before you begin to make the recipes in this book, take a few minutes to master some simple kitchen safety rules.

> ✔ *Ask an adult to be your assistant chef. To ensure your safety, some steps in a recipe are best done with the help of an adult, like handling pots of boiling water or hot cooking oils. Good cooking is about teamwork. With an adult assistant to help, you've got the makings of a perfect team.*

> ✔ *Read the entire recipe before you start to prepare it and have a clear understanding of how the recipe works. If something is not clear, ask your teammate to explain it.*

> ✔ *Dress the part of a chef. Wear an apron. Tie back long hair so that it's out of your food and away from open flames. Why not do what a chef does and wear a clean hat to cover your hair!*

> ✔ *Always start with clean hands and a clean kitchen before you begin any recipe. Leave the kitchen clean when you're done.*

> ✔ *Pot holders and hot pads are your friends. The hands they save may be your own. Use them only if they are dry. Using wet holders on a hot pot can cause a serious burn!*

> ✔ *Keep the handles of the pots and pans turned toward the middle of the stove. That way you won't accidentally hit them and knock over pots of hot food. Always use pot holders to open or move a pan on the stove or in the oven.*

> ✔ *Remember to turn off the stove and oven when you are finished cooking. Sounds like a simple idea, but it's easy to forget.*

✔ *A simple rule about knife safety is that your hands work as a team. One hand grips the handle and operates the knife while the other guides the food you are cutting. The hand holding the food should never come close to the blade of the knife. Keep the fingertips that hold the food slightly curved and out of the path of the blade, and use your thumb to keep the food steady. Go slowly. There is no reason to chop very fast.*

✔ *Always hold the knife handle with **dry** hands. If your hands are wet, the knife might slip. Work on a cutting board, never a tabletop or countertop.*

✔ *Never place sharp knives in a sink full of soapy water, where they could be hidden from view. Someone reaching into the water might get hurt.*

✔ *Take good care of your knives. Good chef knives should be washed by hand, never in a dishwasher.*

COOKING TERMS

If you've only tasted Mexican fast food, then you don't really know the cooking of Mexico. More and more people today are discovering the pleasures of Mexican cooking and just how inviting and satisfying it is to share real Mexican food with family and friends. The recipes of Mexico—an enticing assortment of satisfying flavors and exciting ingredients—just make you feel like celebrating.

When shopping for ingredients, think fresh! Mexican cooking is all about choosing, preparing, and blending excellent full-flavored and subtle ingredients. The result is pure Mexican flavor magic.

A large number of Mexican dishes are created with sauces. The modern Mexican chef achieves smooth sauces with the use of a blender. With the help of your adult assistant chef and the recipe instructions in this book, you will be able to create the authentic flavors of Mexico in your kitchen.

Here are a few simple cooking techniques to keep in mind as you prepare the recipes in this book:

Reduce   *To boil a liquid at a high temperature until it has partly evaporated. Reducing is used to thicken sauces without having to add any extra fat or flour.*

Sauté   *To lightly fry ingredients in a small amount of fat, butter, or oil, while stirring with a spoon or spatula.*

Simmer　　*To cook food in a liquid kept at just below the boiling point. Gentle bubbles will roll lazily to the top of the liquid that is simmering.*

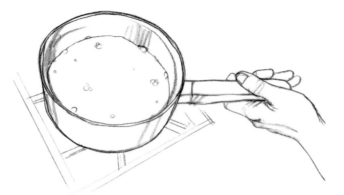

Skim　　*To remove fats or cooking residues as ingredients go from raw to cooked. In making soups or sauces, skimming is an important step in reducing fat and enriching flavor.*

The Regions of Mexico and How They Taste

Mexican food is one of the most popular cuisines in the world. It remains purely Mexican even though several different cultures have introduced ingredients and culinary influences over thousands of years. The most consistent ingredient may be the pride the Mexican cook takes in preparing the dishes of Mexico and sharing them with friends and family.

Officially called the United Mexican States, Mexico is an impressive landmass covering more than 750,000 square miles. Its thirty-one states are home to some 100 million people. Mexico is a mixture of majestic ruins, remote villages, modern industrial centers, and cosmopolitan Mexico City, the largest metropolitan area in the world.

Mexico is part of a region around the Pacific Ocean called the "Ring of Fire." Volcanoes and earthquakes are common here. The scenic Baja California and Yucatán Peninsulas, rainforests, deserts, dazzling seashores, and awesome mountain ranges make this land a geological wonder. Remarkable food, an appealing climate, and some of the world's most beautiful beaches along the Gulf of Mexico, Caribbean Sea, Pacific Ocean, and Gulf of California make Mexico a favorite vacation spot.

Mexico's contributions to the world's table have been significant. It was in Mexico and neighboring Guatemala that, centuries ago, the wild corn plant was successfully cultivated into a high-yielding domestic crop. That golden beauty is now the third most important crop in the world, after wheat and rice. Other foods that have become favorites worldwide, such as vanilla, tomatoes, chiles, and chocolate, also came from Mexico.

There is always a reason to celebrate in Mexico. Family and friends come together to honor Mexican traditions on national holidays. The Feast of the Epiphany (January 6), Cinco de Mayo (May 5), Mexican Independence Day (September 16), the Day of the Dead (November 1 and 2), and a number of saints' feast days are all official reasons for a fiesta. Across the country, Mexicans take part in preparing for and celebrating these holidays. Feasts, fireworks, kaleidoscopic costumes, and the music of the mariachis (Mexican street bands) make these traditional festivals truly spectacular.

The Mexicans have created a special style of cooking just for festivals, or so it

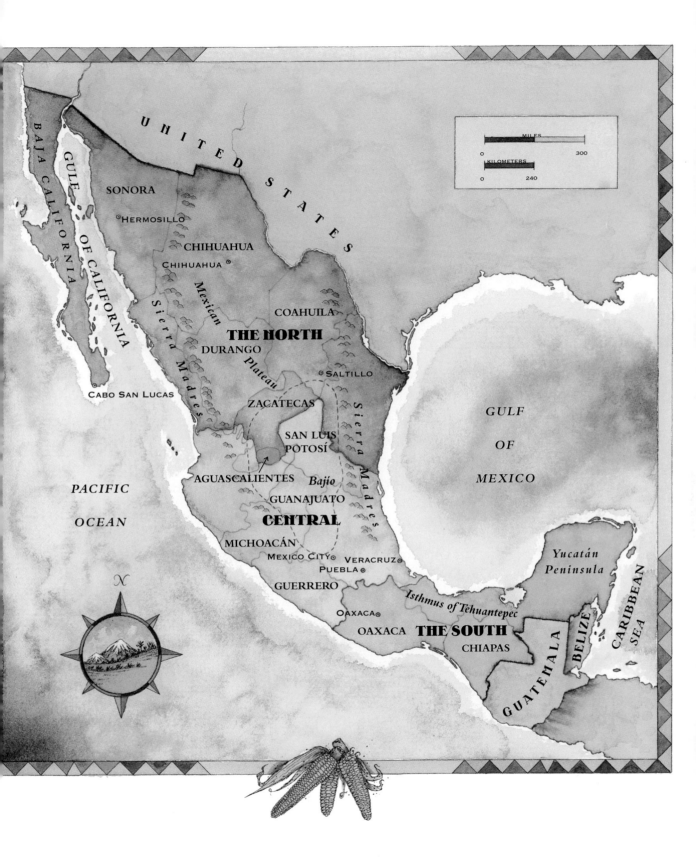

The landscape of northern Mexico includes starkly beautiful deserts and jagged mountain chains.

seems. *Antojitos* are an assortment of snacks eaten out of the hands. A familiar sight all over Mexico are the street vendors selling favorite *antojito* treats such as tacos, crispy tortillas, tamales, and the giant stuffed sandwiches on hard rolls called *tortas*. A fresh fruit drink called *agua fresca* is refreshing after sampling spicy roasted corn on the cob with chiles and a squeeze of fresh lime. Sliced watermelon, cantaloupe, and pineapple are carried in small bags and nibbled as celebrants take in the festivities.

    The Cooking of Mexico is a collection of favorite Mexican dishes, some of which you will recognize and others that might surprise you. There is even a section of recipes to help you create a *taquisa*—a taco party. For simplicity, we have divided the cooking of Mexico into three culinary regions: the north, central Mexico, and the south.

THE NORTH

El Norte, as the Mexicans call it, begins at the southern border of the United States. The Sierra Madres—a rugged mountain system formed out of shale and limestone—extend southward from this region, following the coastlines of the Pacific Ocean and the Gulf of Mexico. Between these mountain fringes is the vast Mexican plateau.

    The northern landscape of Mexico is beautiful, desolate, and forbidding. Stark deserts, salt flats, snowcapped mountains, colorful citrus groves, and dramatic coast-lines create an ever-changing landscape. The Baja California Peninsula, on the Pacific, features world-famous resort cities such as Cabo San Lucas.

Across from the leg of the peninsula are the largest states in Mexico—Sonora, Coahuila, Chihuahua, and Durango. These states are a mix of industrial cities and cattle ranches. Cowboys are a familiar sight on the parched plains of El Norte, which is often referred to as the "frontier." Visitors will also see factory workers in straw hats, boots, and blue jeans on the streets of cities including Hermosillo and Chihuahua.

This is also dairy country. Local farmers produce a special cheese called *queso fundido,* which is used to stuff green *poblano* chiles before roasting. The wheat that is grown here often ends up in the flour tortillas that are a popular part of northern cuisine. Rich cream mixed with mild chiles is spread on tortillas and rolled into delicious handheld snacks. Anaheim chiles are popular because of their mild flavor and subtle heat. The salsa *pico de gallo,* a blend of tomatoes, onions, and chiles, is a constant accompaniment to meals.

The cooking in the north is simpler and less spicy than in the other regions of Mexico. The ranch-style cooking of cowboys, with its hearty portions, is legendary in the north, and cooking over open fires is common. This fire-roasting adds a rugged, natural character to the flavor of local dishes. Popular dishes include beef stews flavored with tomatoes, onions, and chiles; enchiladas filled with grilled beef; and cowboy beans cooked with chiles.

For a taste of the north, try: Mexican Sauce *(Salsa Pico de Gallo).*

CENTRAL MEXICO

The stark landscape of the north changes drastically as you enter central Mexico. Look around and you will see rich fertile land, rolling green hills, and blossoming trees. The climate is milder and less changeable than in the north. Even though this region may receive less than forty inches of rain a year, it is Mexico's agricultural center. Oxen plow the earth and prepare the soil for planting, and effective irrigation helps crops thrive. Central Mexico is also the most heavily populated area of the country, and has been so for thousands of years. It is a land of sharp contrasts and diversity, with modern and ancient cultures combining in a way that is uniquely Mexican.

A visitor to the *bajío*—the central region's fertile and historic lowlands—will see ancient towns where European-style churches and cathedrals stand as stately

A marketplace in Mexico City bursts with the bright colors of chiles, tomatoes, melons, and other fresh fruits and vegetables.

reminders of Mexico's sixteenth-century Spanish conquerors. In the state of Zacatecas are found Spanish-style mansions that once were home to silver tycoons. Shoppers stroll through multicolored marketplaces among baskets and sacks of chiles, squash blossoms, cactus pads, sweet potatoes, and avocados and other tropical fruits. Tolucan Indian produce sellers offer exotic fruits and vegetables.

Exceptional local recipes have deep culinary roots in central Mexico. Cooks in the state of San Luis Potosí are famous for their combination of pork in a peanut sauce spiced with chiles. To the southwest, in Aguascalientes, enchiladas are stuffed with chicken that has been simmered in stock and cooked in a mild ancho chile sauce, then topped with a freshly made local cheese.

The Spaniards introduced the Mexicans to many unfamiliar ingredients, and Mexican cooks found new and inviting ways to use them. Sugar, rice, almonds, raisins, pork, beef from Spanish cattle, butter, milk, cheese, and spices including cinnamon and nutmeg all eventually found a place in the Mexican kitchen. The Mexicans added these new ingredients to their own traditional recipes. *Picadillo,* from Puebla, southeast of Mexico City, is a perfect example. Mexican cooks combined almonds, raisins, and other new ingredients from Spain to create this subtly spiced ground meat filling for tacos and tortillas.

In the state of Michoacán, the candies are legendary. But most renowned of all Mexican desserts may be rice pudding. A specialty of the state of Guanajuato, rice pudding is a uniquely Mexican blend of Spanish and traditional native Mexican ingredients.

Mexico City and its surrounding area, home to more than 16 million people, is like the perfect Mexican recipe. It combines many ingredients, some traditional and some very contemporary, into one amazing creation. Ultramodern, cosmopolitan, and beautiful, the city has thousands of restaurants. You will find elegant establishments serving the new cooking of Mexico, international restaurants, and traditional local restaurants almost side by side.

It isn't only in Mexico City's restaurants that one finds something scrumptious to eat. Street vendors are everywhere. Throughout the many neighborhoods of this sprawling city, tasty snacks such as tortillas with an assortment of fillings, topped with zesty salsas, are sold on the street. Marketplaces with eye-popping displays of colorful chiles, tropical fruits, and tempting tacos and tamales ask every visitor the same question: what are you going to taste first?

Southeast of Mexico City, along the coast of the Gulf of Mexico, the aroma of coffee and the sweet fragrance of tropical fruits fill the air. Here you will find the city of Veracruz, where the culinary influences of Spain, Africa, and France are evident in the local cooking style. Maybe that's why Veracruz is such a popular place to visit. People come for the festivals and the food, especially for the seafood dishes that are famous worldwide. Red Snapper from Veracruz in particular is legendary. This dish combines Spanish and Mexican ingredients in a delicious recipe with a well-deserved reputation.

For a taste of central Mexico, try: Red Snapper from Veracruz, Shrimp in Pumpkin Seed Sauce, Red Enchiladas, Ground Meat Filling for Tortillas, Little Pork, and Rice Pudding.

THE SOUTH

Just 125 miles southeast of Veracruz is the Isthmus of Tehuantepec, the narrowest section in Mexico. Here rocky cliffs form natural partitions among the states of Guerrero, Chiapas, and Oaxaca. The valleys below are made rich by rainfall so abundant that it is measured in feet rather than inches.

Though the distance from Veracruz is short, this ancient region is very much removed from that city's lively air. It is in these fertile valleys that the Huave Indians have preserved their ancient folklore, language, native dress, and recipes. Their culture is an example of how Mexico's indigenous people have kept their traditions alive in spite of the impact of recent oil discoveries across the south and along the Pacific and Gulf coasts.

The state of Oaxaca, at the center of the southern highlands, is regarded by many as the best place to experience Mexican cooking. The terrain here is rugged, and there are no modern highways. Isolation has helped the native people preserve their social and culinary traditions. That may be why the cooking of Oaxaca is so highly regarded throughout the rest of the country.

One example of the local specialties is chicken simmered with ground almonds in a mildly flavored chile sauce. The local cheese, which is stringy and twisted into small ropes, is melted and served hot and delicious with grilled chiles.

In the heart of Oaxaca's capital city, also called Oaxaca, you can hear music from local bandstands as you enjoy colonial architecture from the time of the Spanish. A favorite pastime is to sit at sidewalk cafés and indulge in the guacamole

Appetizing fresh fruits and just-picked vegetables are on sale at an outdoor market in the southern city of Oaxaca.

that is made from local avocados. This is appetizingly prepared in *molcajetes*—volcanic stone bowls that have been used for centuries to crush and grind ingredients.

For a taste of the south, try: Chicken in Almond Sauce, and Zucchini with Corn and Tomatoes.

Mexican cooking is more than just a few popular recipes. The cooking of Mexico is subtle, complex, and deeply satisfying. The rest of the world is beginning to discover what the people of Mexico already know—if the menu is Mexican, the food will be outstanding!

Buen provecho (good eating)!

Soups, Salsas, & Snacks

Clockwise from the top: *Tortilla Chips (page 28), Green Salsa (page 25), Avocado Dip (page 30), and Mexican Sauce (page 27)*

Chicken Stock *Caldo de Pollo*

To make authentic Mexican dishes, you might start with an authentic homemade chicken stock. You can buy canned stock, and that works pretty well in most recipes. Making your own chicken stock, however, adds great flavor and is an excellent way to control the amount of sodium in your finished dish.

Makes 1/2 gallon

Ingredients

1 whole chicken, preferably organic/free-range
   (3 1/2 pounds)
12 cups cold water
1 large white onion
2 cloves garlic
1 bay leaf
1 teaspoon dried basil

2 whole cloves
3 whole black peppercorns
1 stalk celery
3 carrots
1 teaspoon salt

On your mark, get set . . .

- **Rinse the chicken in cold running water. Remove the chicken parts from the inside.**
- **Place the chicken and chicken parts in a 4-quart stockpot on the stove and add 12 cups cold water.**
- **Cut the onion into quarters (don't peel it). Crush the garlic cloves (leave the skins on).**
- **Add the onion and garlic to the stockpot.**
- **Rinse the celery and carrots and cut into large pieces. Add to the stockpot along with the rest of the ingredients.**

Cook!

- **Bring the pot to a boil on medium-high heat.**
- **Reduce the heat to low and simmer for about 1 1/2 hours. Skim off the gray foam that rises to the surface of the stock as it cooks.**
- **When the chicken is cooked, turn off the heat. Get help from an adult assis-**

tant to strain the stock through a metal colander lined with cheesecloth, into another pot or large heatproof bowl. Discard the vegetables and spices.

- Let the chicken cool completely in the colander.
- When the chicken is cool, remove and discard the skin, pull the meat from the bones, and place it in a clean bowl. Cover the chicken and refrigerate. The chicken can be used in salads, sandwiches, and recipes that call for cooked chicken.
- Let the strained stock cool, uncovered, for about 20 minutes. Cover and refrigerate. The fat that rises to the top of the stock after it has cooled should be removed and discarded.
- You have now made pure Mexican chicken stock!

CHEF'S TIP

The finished chicken stock will keep for up to one week in the refrigerator in an airtight container, or it can be poured into smaller plastic containers with tight-fitting lids and frozen for up to three months. To thaw frozen chicken stock, place the container upside down under cold running water and press the bottom to push out the frozen stock. Place the frozen stock in a pan on the stove, cover, and heat on low heat until the stock melts. Chicken stock can also be thawed overnight in the refrigerator. Never thaw chicken stock on the counter or at room temperature.

Tortilla Soup *Sopa de Tortilla*

What's the perfect thing to do with leftover tortillas? Make tortilla soup, of course. This classic soup of Mexico is so popular that each culinary region has its own version.

Serves 6

Ingredients

4 to 6 leftover corn tortillas
1 medium-size white onion
2 cloves garlic
8 ounces Monterey Jack or Mexican queso fresco cheese
1 lime

1 small ripe tomato or 1/2 cup canned tomatoes, undrained
1/3 cup corn or canola oil
6 cups Chicken Stock, either homemade (page 20) or canned low-sodium
1 dried pasilla or ancho chile

On your mark, get set . .

- Stack the tortillas and cut them into strips about 1/4 inch wide. Let them air-dry on the counter while you prepare the rest of the ingredients.
- Peel and slice the onion into thin slices.
- Peel the garlic and leave whole.
- Cut the cheese into small cubes and set aside.
- Cut the lime into 6 wedges and set aside.
- If using a fresh tomato, wash it and cut out the stem circle at the top. Cut the tomato into quarters. If using canned tomatoes, measure 1/2 cup, undrained.

Cook!

- Heat 1 tablespoon of the oil in a 4-quart heavy-bottomed pot on medium-low heat.
- Add the sliced onion and whole garlic cloves. Cook for 8 to 10 minutes, or until golden brown.
- Ask your adult assistant to help with the next steps.
- Add the cooked onion and garlic along with the tomato to the jar of a blender.
- Press the lid almost completely in place, leaving it slightly ajar. Blend at low speed for a few seconds. Now press the lid firmly in place and blend at high speed for about 10 to 15 seconds, or until liquefied.

- Heat another 1 tablespoon of the oil in the pot for 30 seconds, then pour in the tomato mixture from the blender. Have a lid close by, as the mixture will bubble and boil when it hits the hot oil. Cover the pot for a few seconds to prevent spattering.
- Remove the cover, and stir and cook the tomato mixture on low heat for about 5 minutes as it thickens.
- Add the chicken stock and bring to a boil. Reduce the heat to low and simmer for 20 to 30 minutes.
- In the meantime, heat the remaining oil in a 10-inch frying pan on medium heat.
- Add the tortilla strips, a few at a time, and fry until crispy. Remove with a metal slotted spoon and drain on paper towels. Repeat this step until all the tortilla strips are fried.
- Cut the top off the dried chile and run a knife along the side to open the chile like a book. Remove the seeds and veins.
- Cut the chile into 1-inch-wide strips.
- Reheat the oil on medium heat for 30 to 40 seconds.
- Fry the chile pieces for about 30 seconds to crisp them. Remove the chile and drain on paper towels.
- You are now ready to serve the soup. Add the tortilla strips to the simmering soup. Place a few cheese cubes in each individual bowl. Pour the hot soup on top and serve. Pass the chile strips and lime wedges at the table, and let your guests add them if they wish.

Green Salsa *Salsa Verde*

You have seen it on store shelves and on the tables at Mexican restaurants. Now you can make it at home and experience the real taste treat that is *salsa verde*. Use it to top Red Enchiladas (page 58) or Little Pork (page 40), or alongside a bowl of crispy Tortilla Chips (page 28). However you decide to use it, you will be making this recipe again and again.

Serves 6

Ingredients

2 cloves garlic
1/2 small white onion
1 pound tomatillos
8 to 10 fresh cilantro sprigs

1 or 2 fresh jalapeño peppers (or to taste)
3 cups water
2 teaspoons salt
1 tablespoon corn or canola oil

On your mark, get set . . .

- Peel the garlic and leave whole.
- Peel the onion, chop into small pieces, and set aside.
- Peel off the papery outer husks from the tomatillos. Wash them with cold water.
- Wash the cilantro sprigs and shake to remove excess water. Pat dry and set aside.
- Remove the stems from the jalapeños.

Cook!

- Add the water, garlic cloves, tomatillos, whole jalapeños, and salt to a 3-quart pan.
- Bring to a boil on medium-high heat. Reduce the heat to low and simmer, uncovered, for 10 minutes.
- Drain through a colander, reserving 1/2 cup of the cooking liquid.
- Ask your adult assistant to help with the next steps.
- Add the tomatillo mixture, cilantro, and reserved cooking liquid to the jar of a blender.
- Press the lid almost completely in place, leaving it slightly ajar. Blend at low speed for a few seconds. Now press the lid firmly in place and blend at high speed for about 10 to 15 seconds, or until liquefied.
- Remove the jar from the blender and place it near the stove.
- Heat the oil in a 10-inch frying pan on medium heat for 20 seconds.
- Add the chopped onion. Cook for 4 to 5 minutes, or until the onion begins to brown.
- Remove the pan from the heat and pour in the liquid from the blender. Have a lid close by, as the mixture will bubble and boil when it hits the hot pan. Cover the pan for a few seconds to prevent spattering.
- Remove the cover and cook on low heat for about 5 minutes, stirring occasionally.
- Let cool completely and serve.

BROOKLYN AVENUE LIBRARY
VALLEY STREAM UFSD #24
VALLEY STREAM, NY 11582

Mexican Sauce *Salsa Pico de Gallo*

Did you know that salsa outsells ketchup as the most popular condiment in the United States? What makes salsa so popular is its fresh taste. It goes so well with just about everything. You may be tempted to make this popular sauce recipe in a blender, but don't—the end result will be more like salsa soup. Mexican Sauce is best made about one hour before you are ready to serve it, so its flavor can come to life.

Serves 6

Ingredients

3 medium-size ripe tomatoes or 4 or 5 Roma tomatoes (about 1 1/2 pounds)
1 to 3 fresh serrano or jalapeño peppers (or to taste)
1 small white onion

10 to 12 sprigs fresh cilantro
1 lime
1 teaspoon salt

On your mark . . .

- Wash the tomatoes and remove the stem circle at the top.
- Cut the tomatoes in half, then cut each half into 1/4-inch-thick slices.
- Cut the slices into small chunks and, using a spoon, scoop up the tomatoes into a medium-size bowl.

Get set . . .

- Slip on a pair of rubber or latex kitchen gloves.
- Slice the stem end off the peppers. Cut the peppers in half lengthwise. Rinse out the seeds and discard.
- Finely chop or mince the peppers and add to the tomatoes. Rinse the gloves and remove them.
- Peel and finely chop the onion, measure 1/2 cup, and add to the tomatoes.
- Wash the sprigs of cilantro and shake off the excess water. Put the sprigs back into a bunch and chop them. Add to the bowl.
- Cut the lime in half and squeeze the juice into the tomato mixture. Add the salt.
- Mix the ingredients together, cover, and let the salsa rest for about 1 hour.

Serve!

- Place in your favorite bowl and serve together with tortilla chips and green salsa.

Tortilla Chips *Tostadas*

Most of us are familiar with the tortilla chips sold in our local supermarket. In Mexico it is much more common to make these crispy chips fresh at home. Once you try your first batch of homemade Tortilla Chips, you might wonder why you've never made these delicious chips before. This recipe offers two ways to cook the chips—frying or baking. The baked ones are lower in fat and just as delicious. Whichever method you choose, be sure to have on hand lots of Guacamole (page 30), Green Salsa (page 25), or Mexican Sauce (page 27) to scoop up and enjoy.

Makes 72 chips

Ingredients

12 corn tortillas
3⁄4 cup canola oil (for frying)
salt to taste (optional)

On your mark . . .

- On a cutting board, place 6 of the tortillas on top of each other like a stack of pancakes.
- Repeat with the remaining 6 tortillas, making 2 stacks.
- Cut each stack in half, then cut each half into 3 wedges.

Get set . . .

- Spread out all the wedges on a clean tray. Cover them loosely with a clean towel and let them dry for about 20 to 30 minutes.

Cook!

TO FRY THE CHIPS:

- You will need a large metal slotted spoon and paper towels. Have your adult assistant handle the frying.
- Place a 10- to 12-inch heavy-bottomed or cast-iron frying pan on the stove and add the oil. It should be about 1 inch deep in the frying pan; if not, add more oil.
- Heat the oil on medium to medium-high heat for 3 to 4 minutes, or until a deep-fry thermometer reads 380°F.

- Add a small handful of the tortilla wedges to the hot oil. Stir carefully with the slotted spoon to keep them moving and separate. The chips will turn light brown and crispy; this will take about 1 minute.
- Remove the chips with the metal slotted spoon and drain them on paper towels. If you are salting the chips, this is the time to sprinkle it on.
- Repeat until all the chips are fried and salted.
- Place the chips in a basket or bowl and serve.

TO BAKE THE CHIPS:

- You will need a baking tray and 2 wire cooling racks. **Preheat the oven to 350°F.**
- Place a cooling rack on the baking tray and spread some of the wedges over it in a single layer. Place the other rack upside down on the wedges to prevent them from curling.
- Bake the wedges for 12 to 15 minutes, or until crispy.
- Remove the tray from the oven. If you are salting the chips, this is the time to sprinkle it on.
- Repeat until all the chips are baked and salted.
- Place the chips in a basket or bowl and serve.

Avocado Dip *Guacamole*

Guacamole is a recipe believed to have come from the ancient Aztec and Maya peoples. It's so popular today that it can be found on almost all Mexican restaurant menus. In Mexico this dip is commonly prepared in a *molcajete,* a bowl made from volcanic stone. Don't worry if you don't own one—a bowl and fork will work just as well. Follow this recipe exactly the first time, and then decide whether you want to use more or less of the pepper and salt to suit your taste. You can read about avocados in the Essential Ingredients section at the back of this book.

Serves 6

Ingredients

1/2 small white onion
1 clove garlic
1 small fresh jalapeño or serrano pepper
*   (or to taste)*
1 medium-size ripe tomato
4 or 5 sprigs fresh cilantro

1 lime
3 ripe Hass avocados
1 teaspoon salt (or to taste)
crispy Tortilla Chips (page 28) to serve

On your mark . . .

- **Peel and finely chop the onion and garlic and place them in a medium-size bowl.**
- **Slip on a pair of rubber or latex kitchen gloves.**
- **Slice the stem end off the pepper and cut the pepper in half lengthwise. Rinse out the seeds under cold running water and discard.**
- **Finely chop the pepper and add to the bowl. Rinse the gloves and remove them.**
- **Wash the tomato and remove the stem circle from the top. Chop the tomato into small chunks. Add them to the bowl, making sure to add any tomato liquid that may have escaped.**
- **Rinse the fresh cilantro, shake off the excess water, and pat dry with paper towels. Chop the cilantro and add to the bowl.**
- **Cut the lime in half and squeeze the juice into a small bowl. Measure 3 tablespoons and add to the tomato mixture.**
- **Toss together all the ingredients and set aside.**

Get set . . .

- About 30 minutes before you are ready to serve the guacamole, prepare the avocados.
- To do this, lay an avocado on a cutting board. With the tip of a sharp knife, start at the stem end and cut all the way around the avocado. Remember that there is a large pit inside, so don't try to cut through it.

- Now pick up the avocado and, holding it with both hands, twist each half in opposite directions to separate the halves. Scoop out the pit with a tablespoon, but don't throw it away.
- Scrape the pulp of the avocado away from the skin and add it to the bowl with the tomato mixture.
- Repeat with the remaining avocados. Add the salt.
- Gently mash the avocados with a wooden spoon or a fork, combining all the ingredients. Don't overmash the guacamole; it should be chunky.
- Put the pits in the bowl. This will keep the dip from changing color.
- Cover the guacamole with a sheet of plastic wrap pressed directly on the surface until ready to serve.

Serve!

- Remove the pits, if you like, and place the dip in a serving bowl.
- Surround the dip with crispy Tortilla Chips and serve immediately.

A Taco Party!

All the ingredients for a complete Taco Party (page 34)

A Taco Party *Taquisa*

It's time for a *taquisa*—a taco party! It's just the right way to show off a few of your Mexican recipes and celebrate a special occasion at the same time. You can do most of the preparation ahead of time, and the ingredients for tacos are easy to make and fun to eat. Forget about buying those boxed tortilla shells from the supermarket. Instead, make your own crispy or soft tortillas. Your guests will enjoy putting together their own tacos, and you will be able to join the fun. To add an authentic touch to your party, don't forget to have plenty of Refried Beans (page 48), White Rice (page 46), and Fresh Fruit Coolers (page 70) on hand.

Serves 6

Ingredients

1 small head romaine or iceberg lettuce
1 pound Mexican queso blanco, Monterey Jack,
   or Cheddar cheese
24 corn tortillas
1/2 cup canola or corn oil for frying tortillas

Taco fillings (prepare at least 2)
1 recipe Chicken Breasts in Stock (page 37)
1 recipe Little Pork (page 40)
1 recipe Ground Meat Filling for Tortillas (page 38)
1 recipe Guacamole (page 30)

Salsa (prepare at least 1)
1 recipe Mexican Sauce (page 27)
1 recipe Green Salsa (page 25)

On your mark, get set . . .

- **Remove any brown or dark leaves from the lettuce. Cut off the stem end and discard.**
- **Wash the lettuce under cold running water to remove any dirt. Drain to remove excess water.**
- **Cut the lettuce in half lengthwise and then cut crosswise into thin strips. Refrigerate the lettuce.**
- **Grate the cheese and put in a serving bowl.**
- **Place the tortillas on a plate. Measure the oil and set aside.**
- **Select the taco fillings from the list. A good rule to follow is that each guest will probably want about 1/4 cup filling for each taco he or she makes.**
- **The salsa, lettuce, and cheese can be at room temperature or cold. The meat**

fillings should be hot. If you are serving Refried Beans and White Rice, they should also be served hot. The tortillas should be served warm.

Cook...

TO MAKE CRISPY TORTILLAS:

- **Preheat the oven to 200°F.**
- Line a metal baking sheet with paper towels and place it in the oven. Be careful not to place the paper towels near the heating element.
- Line a second, smaller metal tray with paper towels and place it next to the stove.
- Heat a frying pan with 2 tablespoons of the oil on medium heat.
- Fry the tortillas, one at a time, for about 1 1/2 minutes on each side, turning them with a pair of tongs.
- Remove each tortilla as it starts to get crispy and brown slightly.
- Lay the hot tortilla on the tray next to the stove and, still using the tongs, fold it in half. After a minute or two, place the crispy tortillas in the oven to keep warm.

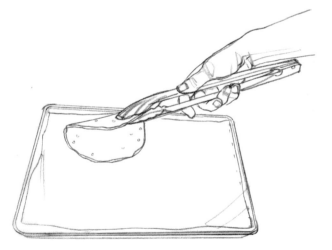

- Repeat this step, adding more oil to the pan as needed, until you have made all the tortillas into crispy shells.

TO MAKE SOFT TORTILLAS:

- Lay a stack of up to 12 tortillas in a clean, heavy kitchen towel and wrap securely.
- Put a pan large enough to hold the tortillas on the stove. Add 1/2 inch water.
- Place a metal vegetable steamer over the water and make sure it's not touching the water.

- Lay the wrapped stack of tortillas in the steamer. If preparing 24 tortillas, use a pan and metal rack large enough to hold the stacks side by side.

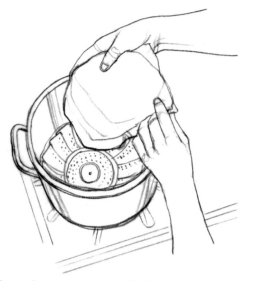

- Cover the pan and bring the water to a boil. Let it boil for 1 minute.
- Turn off the heat. Without opening the pan, let it sit for at least 15 to 20 minutes.
- Serve the tortillas warm.
- You can keep the tortillas warm by simply returning the pan with the wrapped tortillas to the heat and boiling for 1 minute every hour. Or you can place the covered steamer, after it has boiled, in a 200°F oven and keep the tortillas warm for up to 1 hour.

Serve!

- To make it easy for your guests, arrange the fillings, shredded lettuce, cheese, and tortillas all within easy reach.
- If you have a food-warming tray, this is a great time to use it to keep the meats, rice, and beans warm as your party goes on. If you don't have a warming tray, foods can be kept warm on the stove and served in covered dishes.
- Keep your eye on the serving table and refill your dishes as they run low. Most importantly, have fun!

Chicken Breasts in Stock *Pechugas de Pollo*

This recipe is a quick way to prepare chicken breasts for tacos or enchiladas. You can substitute chicken thighs or try a combination of both. The broth that is left after cooking the chicken is excellent for using in soups or sauces, so be sure to save it.

Serves 4

Ingredients

1 carrot
1 stalk celery
1 clove garlic
1 small bunch fresh parsley
2 chicken breasts with bone and skin, preferably organic/free-range (about 10 ounces)

4 cups water
1/2 small white onion
1 teaspoon salt
freshly ground black pepper to taste

On your mark, get set . . .

- Wash, but don't peel, the carrot and celery and coarsely chop.
- Crush and peel the garlic.
- Wash the parsley in cold water.

Cook!

- Put the chicken in a 4-quart stockpot with the rest of the ingredients and bring to a boil.
- Reduce the heat to low and simmer for 35 to 40 minutes, or until the chicken is tender and cooked through to the bone. Skim off any foam that rises to the surface during cooking.
- Drain the chicken through a strainer, reserving the stock. Discard the vegetables.
- Completely cool the stock and refrigerate it for another recipe. Chicken stock will keep for 1 week in the refrigerator or up to 3 months in the freezer.
- After the chicken has cooled, remove the skin and discard. Pull the meat from the bone.
- Shred the chicken into long strips. It is now ready for use in tacos or enchiladas.

Ground Meat Filling for Tortillas *Picadillo*

Picadillo is one of Mexico's many culinary treasures. A warm tortilla stuffed with this sweet and lightly spiced filling is irresistible. *Picadillo* can be used in tacos, enchiladas, or as a stuffing for zucchini or other vegetables. This recipe can be made with a combination of ground pork and beef, or you can choose to use all beef or all pork.

Serves 4 to 6

Ingredients

2 dried ancho chiles
1/2 cup hot water
1 medium-size white onion
2 large ripe tomatoes or 1 cup canned chopped Italian plum tomatoes
2 cloves garlic
10 to 12 pimiento-stuffed olives
1 teaspoon ground cinnamon
1/4 teaspoon ground cloves
1/2 cup raisins
1/2 cup slivered almonds
1/2 teaspoon freshly ground black pepper
1 teaspoon salt
1 teaspoon brown sugar
2 tablespoons olive or vegetable oil
1 pound ground beef (sirloin or top round)
1/3 cup chicken stock or water

On your mark, get set . . .

- Place the ancho chiles in a bowl, cover with 1/2 cup hot water, and let stand for 15 minutes.
- Peel and coarsely chop the onion and measure 1 cup.
- If using fresh tomatoes, wash them and cut out the stem circle at the top. Chop the tomatoes into chunks and measure 1 cup.
- If using canned tomatoes, drain them and measure 1 cup.
- Peel and chop the garlic. Chop the olives.
- Measure the cinnamon, cloves, raisins, almonds, black pepper, salt, and brown sugar and set aside.

Cook!

- Heat a 10- to 12-inch frying pan with the oil on medium-high heat for 30 seconds.
- Add the ground meat and sauté for 4 to 5 minutes, or until the meat is no longer pink, breaking it up with a spoon or spatula as it cooks.
- Using a slotted spoon, remove the meat to a bowl and keep close by.

- Remove the chiles from the soaking water and squeeze out the excess liquid, but do not discard it. Remove the stems and coarsely chop the chiles.
- Reheat the frying pan on medium-high heat for 30 seconds.
- Add the onion, chopped chiles, chile soaking liquid, garlic, and chopped olives. Cook for 3 to 4 minutes.
- Reduce the heat to medium. Add the tomatoes and chicken stock and cook for 5 minutes, stirring occasionally.
- Return the meat to the frying pan.
- Add the cinnamon, cloves, raisins, almonds, black pepper, salt, and brown sugar. Stir well to combine all the ingredients.
- Cover the pan, reduce the heat to low, and simmer for 8 to 10 minutes. Serve hot.

Little Pork *Carnitas*

These "Little Meats" are so popular all over Mexico that each region has its own version. This recipe is from Uruapan in the state of Michoacán in central Mexico. These delicate little chunks of pork are just the right thing to put inside tacos or Red Enchiladas (page 58), or to enjoy on their own as a great lunch or dinner. Spoon on some homemade Green Salsa (page 25) and you have something so tasty you may call them anything but "little."

Serves 6

Ingredients

1 small white onion
2 cloves garlic
2 pounds boneless pork loin end, with a little fat
1 1/2 teaspoons salt

1 teaspoon dried oregano
8 cups cold water
1 large fresh orange
1/2 cup whole milk
2 tablespoons canola oil

On your mark, get set . . .

- Peel the onion and cut into large chunks. Peel and chop the garlic.
- Cut the pork into 2-inch cubes, leaving a small amount of fat on each piece.
- Measure the salt and oregano and set aside.

Cook!

- Place the onion, garlic, pork cubes, water, salt, and oregano in a 6-quart heavy-bottomed pan with a lid.
- Cover the pan and bring the mixture to a boil on medium heat.
- Reduce the heat to medium-low and simmer for about 1 hour, or until the pork is tender but not falling apart.
- In the meantime, squeeze the orange and measure 3/4 cup juice. Measure the milk and set aside.
- When the pork is ready, drain the meat through a colander and discard the cooking broth.
- Reheat the pan on medium heat with 1 tablespoon of the oil for about 20 to 30 seconds.
- Add the orange juice and milk. Add the pork.
- Cook, uncovered, for 5 to 10 minutes. As the pork cooks, the liquid will begin to evaporate.

- Add the remaining 1 tablespoon oil and, using a spoon, mix it into the pork as it cooks. Cook for another 5 to 7 minutes. The pork will turn brown and crispy.
- Place a metal colander inside a heatproof bowl and have it ready next to the stove. When the meat is brown and cooked, remove it to the colander to drain.
- Serve hot as a filling for tacos or Red Enchiladas.

CHEF'S TIP

To save time, you can ask the butcher to cut the meat into 2-inch chunks. When choosing pork for this dish, it is important to find a pork loin end cut, which still has some fat on it. This will help keep the pork moist as it cooks. If you choose a leaner cut, the pork may be dry. If you can't find a pork loin end cut, you can use pork shoulder.

Vegetables, Rice, & Beans

Fresh vegetables and chiles bring color and excitement to the Mexican table.

Zucchini with Corn and Tomatoes
Calabacitas con Elote

This recipe comes from Oaxaca, at the southern coastal tip of Mexico. The Mexican cook would probably use fresh corn at the peak of the summer harvest, ripe tomatoes, and fresh-picked zucchini. If corn is not in season, this recipe works almost as well with frozen corn.

Serves 6

Ingredients

1 1/2 pounds fresh zucchini
2 medium-size ripe tomatoes
1 small white onion
1 clove garlic
2 sprigs fresh cilantro

2 ears fresh corn or 1 cup frozen corn
2 tablespoons canola oil
1 teaspoon salt
freshly ground black pepper to taste

On your mark, get set . . .

- Wash and scrub the zucchini very well with a vegetable brush to remove any dirt.
- Cut the zucchini in half lengthwise. Cut the halves lengthwise into 1-inch-thick slices. Cut the slices into cubes. Set aside.
- Remove the stem circle from the top of the tomatoes, chop the tomatoes into small chunks, and set aside. Peel and chop the onion and garlic.
- Wash the sprigs of cilantro to remove any sand and dry with paper towels. Chop and set aside.
- If using fresh corn, remove the kernels from the cob with a sharp knife. Ask your adult assistant to help with this step. If using frozen corn, measure the corn and set aside.

Cook!

- Heat the oil in a 12-inch frying pan on medium heat.
- Add the garlic and onion and cook for 2 to 3 minutes.
- Add the corn and zucchini and cook for 4 to 5 minutes.
- Add the tomatoes and raise the heat to medium-high. Bring the mixture to a fast boil.
- Add the cilantro, salt, and pepper and reduce the heat to low.
- Cover the pan and simmer for 5 to 7 minutes, or until the vegetables are tender but have not lost their color or crunch. Serve hot.

White Rice *Arroz Blanco*

This basic rice has so many different uses in Mexican cooking that you will want to make plenty of it to keep on hand as an authentic addition to your menu.

Serves 4 to 6

Ingredients

1 cup long-grain white rice
1 cup hot water
1 medium-size white onion
1 clove garlic

2 tablespoons canola or olive oil
2 ½ cups Chicken Stock, either homemade (page 20) or canned low-sodium, or water
1 teaspoon salt

On your mark, get set . . .

- Place the rice in a large bowl and cover with the hot water. Let stand for 15 to 20 minutes.
- Pour the rice into a strainer, shake to remove the excess water, and let drain.
- Peel and chop the onion and garlic into small pieces and set aside.

Cook!

- Heat a heavy-bottomed frying pan with the oil on medium heat for 30 seconds.
- Give the rice one more shake and add it to the frying pan. Cook the rice for 4 to 5 minutes, or until all the grains are coated with oil and begin to color slightly.
- Add the onion and garlic. Cook for 8 to 10 minutes, stirring well to keep from sticking.
- Slowly add the broth or water and the salt and bring to a boil. Cook, uncovered, at a gentle boil for another 10 to 12 minutes, or until the liquid is absorbed and tiny air holes cover the surface of the rice.
- Remove the pan from the heat and cover tightly. Set in a warm place for at least 20 minutes.
- When ready to serve, stir the rice with a fork to loosen and separate the grains and serve hot.

Beans Cooked in a Pot *Frijoles de la Olla*

There is nothing quite like the wonderful aroma from a pot of simmering beans. Beans are one of Mexico's essential and deliciously simple ingredients. This classic recipe has been used by Mexican cooks for many years. Traditionally beans were cooked in clay pots called ollas, which were buried in the hot coals of the daily cooking fire. You can always buy canned beans, but when you discover how easy it is to make homemade beans, you just might decide to leave the can opener in the kitchen drawer. This recipe includes directions for making Mexican Refried Beans. You may think that "refried" means the beans are cooked over and over. What it really means is "cooked well" or "thoroughly" until the liquid is gone.

Serves 6

Ingredients

1 pound (2 1/2 cups) pinto, black, navy, or pink beans
6 to 8 cups water
1 small white or yellow onion

1 clove garlic (optional)
2 tablespoons bacon drippings, vegetable oil, or lard
2 teaspoons salt

On your mark . . .

- **Rinse the beans with cold water in a colander.**
- **Shake off the excess water and pour the beans onto a clean tray in a single layer. Carefully check for and remove any tiny stones or shriveled, very dark beans.**
- **Place the beans in a 4-quart pot and cover with enough water to come 1 inch over the top of the beans.**

Get set . . .

- **Peel and chop the onion into small chunks.**
- **Peel and chop the garlic.**

Cook!

- **Place the pot of beans on medium heat. Add the onion, garlic, and bacon drippings or other fat, and bring to a boil.**
- **Partially cover the beans, reduce the heat to low, and cook at a gentle simmer for 1 1/2 to 2 hours, or until very tender. Now and then check the level of water in the pot. Make sure it stays about 1 inch over the top of the beans. If you need to add water, add hot water only, to keep from stopping the cooking process.**
- **When the beans are tender and almost completely cooked, add the salt and cook, uncovered, for another 10 to 15 minutes.**
- **Turn off the heat and let the beans cool completely.**

- When ready to serve, reheat the beans gently on medium-low heat, stirring occasionally, until bubbly hot. Serve in bowls.

REFRIED BEANS *Frijoles Refritos*

Serves 6 to *8*

Ingredients

1 small white onion
4 cups cooked pinto, black, navy, or pink beans (canned or fresh), undrained
2 tablespoons vegetable or canola oil, bacon or sausage drippings, or lard

2 teaspoons salt (optional)
1/2 cup grated Monterey Jack, feta, Parmesan, or crumbled Mexican queso fresco cheese
1/2 cup tortilla chips

On your mark, get set . . .

- Peel and chop the onion into small pieces.

Cook!

- Place the beans in a 2- to 4-quart pot on low heat and cook for 15 to 20 minutes, stirring occasionally.
- Heat the oil or other fat in a 10- to 12-inch heavy-bottomed frying pan on medium heat.
- Add the onion and sauté about 8 minutes, or until golden brown, being careful not to let it burn. If the onion browns too fast, reduce the heat to low.
- Remove the beans from the cooking liquid with a slotted spoon and add about one-third of them to the frying pan. Using a round potato masher or the back of a large spoon, carefully mash the beans into a coarse texture.

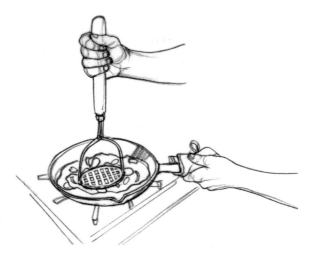

- Add more beans and repeat this step until all the beans are added and coarsely mashed.
- Add 1 cup liquid, either the bean cooking liquid or hot water. Combine the beans and liquid.
- Cook the beans slowly for about 5 to 10 minutes, or until the liquid has almost completely cooked away.
- Taste the beans and add salt if needed. You probably won't need to add any if you are using canned beans.
- Just before serving, check the beans and add more liquid if they are too dry.
- Place the refried beans on a serving platter or in individual bowls, top with the cheese, and garnish with the tortilla chips. Serve hot.

A dish of warm Refried Beans, topped with cheese and ready to eat

Main Dishes

Red Enchiladas (page 58) with White Rice (page 46) and Beans Cooked in a Pot (page 47)

Chicken in Almond Sauce

Pollo en Salsa de Almendras

Chicken in Almond Sauce comes from Oaxaca in the southern region of Mexico, a very exciting place to visit not only for its fascinating beauty but also to sample the local cooking.

Serves 6

Ingredients

3 1/2 pounds chicken, preferably organic/free-range, cut into 8 pieces
2 teaspoons salt
1/4 teaspoon freshly ground black pepper
1 dried pasilla or ancho chile
1/2 cup hot water
1 small white onion
1 clove garlic
2 medium-size ripe tomatoes or 1 cup canned chopped tomatoes

1 lime
1/4 cup vegetable or canola oil
1 teaspoon ground cinnamon or one 2-inch piece stick cinnamon
3 whole black peppercorns
3 whole allspice
1 cup roasted whole almonds
2 cups Chicken Stock, either homemade (page 20) or canned low-sodium

On your mark . . .

- Rinse the chicken pieces in cold water. Pat dry and place in a large bowl.
- Sprinkle with 1 teaspoon of the salt and the black pepper and refrigerate.
- Break the stem top off the chile and discard. Tear the chile into small pieces and place in a bowl. Add the hot water and set aside to soften.

Get set . . .

- Peel and cut the onion into slices. Peel the garlic and leave whole.
- If using fresh tomatoes, wash and cut them into quarters.
- If using canned tomatoes, drain them and measure 1 cup.
- Squeeze the juice from the lime into a small bowl.
- Drain the chile and reserve the soaking liquid.

Cook!

- Heat a 4- to 6-quart heavy-bottomed pan with the oil on low heat.

- Add the onion, garlic, cinnamon, peppercorns, allspice, almonds, and chile. Cook for 8 to 10 minutes, stirring occasionally.
- Ask your adult assistant to help with the next steps.
- Lift the cooked ingredients out of the frying pan with a slotted spoon and place in the jar of a blender along with the tomatoes and the chile soaking liquid.
- Press the lid of the blender almost completely in place, leaving it slightly ajar. Blend at low speed for a few seconds. Now press the lid firmly in place, and blend at high speed for about 30 seconds.
- Pour the blended ingredients into a bowl and add the chicken stock.
- Add the remaining 1 teaspoon salt and stir to combine, then set aside.
- Reheat the pan on medium heat. Add the chicken, a few pieces at a time, and brown on all sides. Remove the browned chicken to a clean platter.
- Ask your adult assistant to drain off all but 1 tablespoon of the oil in the pan. Return the pan to the stove and place on medium heat.
- Pour in the blended ingredients. Have a lid close by to cover the pan for a few seconds to prevent spattering.
- Cook, uncovered, for 10 minutes, stirring occasionally. Add the chicken pieces and lime juice. Spoon the sauce over the chicken.
- Cover the pan and cook on low heat for 35 to 40 minutes, or until the chicken is cooked through to the bone. Serve hot with the sauce.

Red Snapper from Veracruz

Pescado a la Veracruzana

Along the beautiful coastal waters of the Gulf of Mexico is the spectacular city of Veracruz. The Gulf of Mexico has an amazing assortment of seafood. Red snapper is so popular that it frequently gets star billing in local restaurants. This dish is a great example of how the cooking of Spain and Mexico combine to create an international hit that will have you taking the bows.

Serves 4

Ingredients

1 small white onion
2 cloves garlic
2 to 4 canned or fresh jalapeño peppers
4 or 5 sprigs fresh cilantro
½ cup pimiento-stuffed olives
½ teaspoon sugar
½ teaspoon ground cinnamon
¼ teaspoon ground cloves
1 teaspoon salt

1 teaspoon dried oregano
1 lime
2 large ripe tomatoes or 2 cups canned whole plum tomatoes
4 boneless red snapper fillets, about 8 ounces each
¼ cup extra virgin olive oil
1 tablespoon butter

On your mark . . .

- **Peel and chop the onion into small pieces. Peel and chop the garlic.**
- **Slip on a pair of rubber or latex kitchen gloves.**
- **Cut the jalapeños in half, remove the stems and seeds, and chop into small chunks.**
- **Measure 2 tablespoons and set aside. Rinse the gloves and remove them.**
- **Rinse the cilantro sprigs and pat dry with paper towels. Chop the cilantro.**
- **Chop the olives and measure ½ cup.**
- **Measure the sugar, cinnamon, cloves, salt, and oregano and set aside.**
- **Squeeze the juice from half of the lime into a small bowl and measure 1 ½ tablespoons.**

Get set . . .

- **If using fresh tomatoes, wash them and remove the stem circle. Cut the tomatoes into quarters.**
- **If using canned tomatoes, drain them and measure 2 cups.**

- Ask your adult assistant to help with the next step.
- Place the tomatoes in the jar of a blender and press the lid firmly in place. Blend the tomatoes at high speed for 20 seconds to liquefy. Pour into a bowl and set aside.
- Wash the fish fillets and pat dry with paper towels. Lay them in a lightly oiled oven-safe baking dish and keep refrigerated until ready to bake.

Cook!

- **Preheat the oven to 425°F.**
- Place the olive oil in a 3-quart pan on medium-low heat.
- Add the onion, garlic, and jalapeños, and cook for 6 to 8 minutes, or until the onion is very soft.
- Raise the heat to medium. Add the blended tomatoes, cilantro, olives, sugar, cinnamon, cloves, salt, oregano, and lime juice.
- Bring to a boil, then reduce the heat to low. Cook, uncovered, for about 12 minutes.
- Add the butter. Mix well. Remove from the heat and let cool for about 5 to 10 minutes.
- Spread the sauce evenly over the top of the fish fillets and bake for 20 to 25 minutes, basting once.
- Serve hot with rice.

Shrimp in Pumpkin Seed Sauce

Camarones al Pipian

This recipe comes from Tampico, on the Gulf of Mexico, where local cooks prepare gulf shrimp in a colorful and mouthwatering sauce. The recipe blends the Mexicans' love of seafood and pumpkin seeds into a delightful and elegant dish.

Serves 6

Ingredients

1 to 3 fresh serrano or jalapeño peppers (or to taste)
8 to 10 sprigs fresh cilantro
1 small white onion
1 ½ pounds fresh or thawed frozen large shrimp with shells

1 ½ cups water
1 teaspoon salt
freshly ground black pepper to taste
1 cup shelled roasted pumpkin seeds, unsalted
2 tablespoons butter
⅔ cup sour cream

On your mark, get set . . .

- Slip on a pair of rubber or latex kitchen gloves.
- Remove the stems from the peppers and discard. Cut the peppers in half lengthwise.
- Rinse and remove the seeds and white inner membrane and discard. Rinse the gloves and remove them.
- Wash the cilantro, shake off the excess water, and pat dry with paper towels. Chop the cilantro and set aside.
- Peel and chop the onion, measure 1/2 cup, and set aside.

Cook!

- Put the shrimp, with the shells, in a 3- to 4-quart pan.
- Add the water, salt, and black pepper and bring to a boil on medium heat.
- Reduce the heat to low and simmer for 3 to 4 minutes, or until the shrimp just turn pink. Stir the shrimp to help them cook evenly.
- Remove the shrimp with a slotted spoon to a bowl and let cool, reserving the cooking liquid (shrimp broth).
- After the shrimp have cooled, peel and devein them. Place the shells back in the shrimp broth. Refrigerate the shrimp.

- Simmer the shells in the broth, covered, on low heat for 5 to 6 minutes.
- Strain and reserve the broth and discard the shells.
- If the pumpkin seeds are already roasted, you can skip the next step.
- Place a dry cast-iron or heavy-bottomed frying pan on medium heat for about 1 minute. Add the pumpkin seeds and stir them to allow even cooking. The seeds will begin to brown and pop but continue to stir. If they are browning too fast, reduce the heat. Cook for 5 to 6 minutes, or until the seeds are browned and puffed.
- Remove from the heat and empty into a heatproof bowl to cool.
- Ask your adult assistant to help with the next steps.
- Add the shrimp broth, chopped onion, peppers, and cilantro to the jar of a blender. Add the toasted pumpkin seeds. Press the lid almost completely in place, leaving it slightly ajar. Blend at low speed for a few seconds. Now press the lid firmly in place and blend for about 1 minute, or until smooth.
- Melt the butter in a 10- to 12-inch frying pan on low heat. Add the pumpkin seed sauce and cook for about 8 to 10 minutes. Add the shrimp and heat through.
- Stir in the sour cream and mix well.
- Serve hot over rice or with warm corn tortillas.

Red Enchiladas *Enchiladas Rojas*

What dish is more recognizably Mexican than enchiladas? This recipe is from Aguascalientes in the central region of Mexico. Making enchiladas can be messy. Wear an apron, take your time, and most importantly, read the recipe completely to make sure you have everything you need close by.

Serves 6

Ingredients

Sauce
3 medium-size ripe tomatoes or 2 cups canned
    whole tomatoes
2 dried ancho chiles
2 dried pasilla chiles
1 small white onion
1 clove garlic
1 cup hot water
1 tablespoon corn or olive oil
1 1/2 cups Chicken Stock, either homemade
    (page 20) or canned low-sodium
1 teaspoon salt

Enchiladas
2 cups Chicken Breasts in Stock (page 37)
12 corn tortillas
1 cup grated Mexican queso fresco, feta, or
    Monterey Jack cheese

On your mark, get set . . .

- **If using canned tomatoes, drain them, measure 2 cups, and set aside.**
- **Place a dry heavy-bottomed or cast-iron frying pan on medium heat. Lay the whole dried chiles and the whole unpeeled fresh tomatoes, onion, and garlic in the frying pan.**
- **Roast the chiles for 1 to 2 minutes on each side, turning with a pair of tongs.**
- **Remove the chiles and place them in a bowl. Cover with 1 cup hot water and let stand for 20 to 30 minutes.**
- **Cook the rest of the ingredients in the frying pan for another 4 to 5 minutes, turning them occasionally. Don't worry if the tomatoes, onion, and garlic acquire burned spots—that will add great flavor.**
- **Remove the vegetables from the pan and let cool.**
- **Remove the stems and seeds from the soaked chiles and discard. Reserve the soaking liquid.**

- Cut out the stem circle from the cooled tomatoes and discard. Peel the cooled garlic and onion.
- Coarsely chop the tomatoes, onion, and garlic.
- Ask your adult assistant to help you with the next step.
- Place the tomatoes (fresh or canned) in the jar of a blender along with the onion, garlic, chiles, and the chile soaking liquid. Press the lid firmly in place and blend the sauce at high speed until it liquefies. Pour into a bowl.
- Heat 1 tablespoon of the oil in the frying pan on medium heat for 20 seconds.
- Add the sauce. It will bubble and boil, so have a lid close by to cover the pan for a few seconds to prevent spattering.
- Reduce the heat to low. Add the chicken stock and salt to the sauce and cook on low heat for 10 to 15 minutes. Reduce the heat to simmer.

Cook!

- **Preheat the oven to 350°F.**
- Measure 2 cups of the shredded chicken and set aside.
- Warm a tortilla in a dry skillet on low heat for 1 minute on each side, turning it with a pair of tongs. This will soften the tortilla and make it easier to roll. Still using the tongs, dip it into the sauce to completely coat the tortilla. Lay the tortilla on a clean plate.
- Place about 2 1/2 tablespoons of the shredded chicken and about 1 tablespoon of the cheese on the tortilla.
- Roll up the tortilla and place it in a 10-inch baking dish, seam side down. You just made an enchilada!
- Repeat these steps until all the tortillas are warmed and filled.
- Pour the remaining sauce over the top of the completed enchiladas. Sprinkle on the remaining cheese.
- Bake the enchiladas for 4 to 6 minutes, or until the cheese is melted.
- Serve with White Rice (page 46) and Refried Beans (page 48).

Tamale Pie *Tamal de Cazuela*

Tamales are usually made from stone-ground cornmeal and wrapped around an assortment of fillings, then tied in a corn husk and steamed. A little bit of food heaven! This pie is an easier way to enjoy a tamale and its exceptional flavors. Leftover chicken, turkey, pork, beef, vegetables, cheese, and even flavored tofu make great fillings for Tamale Pie. Don't have any leftovers? No problem. Just follow the recipe below, and when your guests are raving about how delicious your Tamale Pie is, tell them you made it from scratch.

Serves 6 to 8

Ingredients

Tamale

3 cups chicken, beef, or vegetable stock, or water
2 tablespoons corn oil, melted butter, or lard
1 cup masa harina or quick-cooking grits (not instant)
1 1/2 teaspoons baking powder
1/2 teaspoon salt
2 eggs

Sauce

1 medium-size ripe tomato or 1 cup canned tomatoes
2 dried ancho chiles
1 dried chipotle chile
1 small white onion
1 clove garlic
1 cup hot water
1/2 cup chicken stock or water

Filling

2 cups cubed cooked chicken, turkey, pork, beef, vegetables, or smoked tofu, or 2 cups Little Pork (page 40), Ground Meat Filling for Tortillas (page 38), or Chicken Breasts in Stock (page 37)
8 ounces Monterey Jack cheese
8 ounces feta cheese

On your mark . . .

- **Bring the stock or water to a boil in a 4-quart pot. Add the oil, butter, or lard.**
- **Combine the masa harina, baking powder, and salt in a bowl.**
- **Carefully pour half of the dry ingredients into the boiling liquid in a steady stream. Stir with a whisk to prevent lumps.**
- **Add the second half of the dry ingredients and stir.**
- **Cook the mixture on low heat for 5 to 10 minutes, stirring frequently to keep it from sticking or burning. Remove from the heat.**

- Add the eggs, one at a time, and mix in thoroughly. The tamale mixture will now resemble a cake batter. It won't be very thick.
- Place the tamale mixture back on low heat and cook for another 2 to 3 minutes, stirring to prevent sticking.
- Remove from the heat and let rest while you prepare the rest of the ingredients.

Get set . . .

- If using canned tomatoes, drain them, measure 1 cup, and set aside.
- Place a dry heavy-bottomed or cast-iron frying pan on medium heat. Lay the whole dried chiles and the whole unpeeled fresh tomato, onion, and garlic in the frying pan.
- Roast the chiles for 1 to 2 minutes on each side, turning with a pair of tongs.
- Remove the chiles, place them in a bowl, and cover with 1 cup hot water. Let stand for 20 to 30 minutes to soften.
- Continue roasting the rest of the ingredients for 4 to 5 minutes, turning them occasionally. Don't worry if the tomato, onion, and garlic acquire burned spots—that will add great flavor.
- Remove the tomato, onion, and garlic from the pan and let cool.
- Peel and chop the onion and measure 1/2 cup. Peel the garlic and leave whole.

- Cut out the stem circle from the tomato and chop the tomato into large chunks.
- Remove the stems and seeds from the soaked chiles and discard. Reserve 1/2 cup of the soaking liquid.
- Ask your adult assistant to help with the next step.
- Place the tomato (fresh or canned) in the jar of a blender along with the onion, garlic, chiles, and chile soaking liquid. Press the lid firmly in place and blend the sauce at high speed for 30 seconds, or until smooth.

- Reheat the frying pan on medium heat for about 1 minute. Pour in the blended sauce. Be prepared with a lid to cover the pan and prevent spattering.
- Reduce the heat to low, remove the lid, and cook for 20 minutes, stirring occasionally. Add the stock or water as needed if the sauce gets too thick.
- Measure 1 1/2 cups sauce and set aside.
- Measure 2 cups meat or vegetable filling and set aside.
- Grate or crumble the cheeses and set aside.

Cook!

- **Preheat the oven to 400°F.**
- Spread half of the tamale mixture over the bottom of a 10-inch round oven-proof casserole or pie dish.
- Spread the meat or vegetable filling and the Monterey Jack cheese over the tamale layer.
- Spoon on the sauce.

- Make the top layer with the rest of the tamale mixture, roughly spreading it to cover the sauce and filling.
- Finish the pie by covering the top with the feta cheese.
- Bake the pie for 1 hour 10 minutes. After 45 minutes, loosely cover the top with a piece of aluminum foil to prevent overbrowning.
- Remove from the oven and let cool for 15 minutes before serving.

CHEF'S TIP

You can save time by using your favorite bottled salsa in this recipe instead of making the sauce.

Desserts & Drinks

Fresh Fruit Coolers (page 70) and
Mexican Celebration Cookies (page 68)

Rice Pudding *Arroz con Leche*

If you were to ask what dessert is the favorite in Mexico, chances are Rice Pudding might be the name you would hear the most. There are many versions of Rice Pudding, but there is only one *arroz con leche*. It's an exceptional dessert.

Serves 6

Ingredients

1 fresh orange
1 cup long-grain white rice
2 1/2 cups water
1 two-inch piece stick cinnamon or
  2 teaspoons ground cinnamon
1 pinch salt

1 egg
1 1/2 cups sugar
4 cups whole milk
1/2 cup dark raisins
1 teaspoon pure vanilla extract
extra ground cinnamon for serving

On your mark, get set . . .

- **Wash the orange.**
- **With a potato peeler, peel off two 3-inch-long strips of the orange skin.**
- **Lay the strips together on a cutting board and carefully mince them into small bits. Measure 1 tablespoon and set aside.**

Cook!

- **In a 3- to 4-quart pan, add the rice, water, cinnamon, minced orange peel, and salt. Bring to a boil on high heat.**
- **Reduce the heat to low, cover, and simmer for 15 minutes, or until the liquid is almost all absorbed.**
- **In the meantime, combine the egg and sugar in a large bowl. Beat with an electric hand mixer at low speed for about 1 minute, or until smooth.**
- **Add the milk and beat for another 30 seconds.**
- **When the rice has cooked for 15 minutes, pour in the egg, milk, and sugar mixture and stir well to combine.**
- **Cook on low heat for 5 minutes, or until the pudding starts to thicken, stirring to prevent it from sticking.**

- Add the raisins and vanilla and cook for another 2 to 3 minutes.
- Remove the pudding from the heat and let cool off the stove, uncovered, for 20 to 25 minutes.
- Spoon the cooled pudding into individual serving dishes or a large serving bowl. Chill completely.
- Serve with ground cinnamon dusted on top.

Mexican Celebration Cookies *Polvorones*

These cookies are popular all over Mexico and are a favorite dessert at weddings and other celebrations. Their name comes from the Spanish word *polvo*, which means "dust," and these sweets are so light and delicate that the name is a perfect fit.

Makes 32 cookies

Ingredients

2 cups all-purpose flour
1 cup confectioners' sugar
1⁄4 teaspoon salt
1 stick unsalted butter, softened

1⁄2 cup vegetable shortening
1 teaspoon pure vanilla extract
1 cup chopped pecans, walnuts, or almonds

On your mark, get set . . .

- Combine the flour, 1⁄2 cup of the confectioners' sugar, and the salt in a large bowl.
- Sift the dry ingredients into another bowl and set aside.
- Place the softened butter, shortening, and vanilla in a large bowl and beat with an electric hand mixer until smooth.
- Add the dry ingredients and nuts. Combine all the ingredients into a rough dough, using a spoon or very clean hands.
- Remove the dough from the bowl and place on a clean, lightly floured surface. Gently knead into a smooth dough.
- Shape into a ball, wrap in plastic wrap, and chill for at least 30 minutes.

Cook!

- **Preheat the oven to 350°F.**
- Cut the chilled dough into quarters. Working with one quarter at a time, using your fingertips, roll each quarter into a 7- to 8-inch-long log.
- Cut each log into 8 pieces.
- Roll 1 piece into a ball between the palms of your hands and place the balls on an ungreased baking sheet, about 1 inch apart.
- Repeat these steps until all the dough is rolled into cookies.
- Place the baking sheet on the middle rack of the oven and bake for 30 minutes, or until lightly browned.

- When the cookies are baked, let cool slightly. Carefully remove the cookies with a spatula to a rack to cool completely.
- Put the remaining 1/2 cup confectioners' sugar in a wide bowl. Roll the cooled cookies in the sugar to evenly coat them, place them on a plate, and serve.

Fresh Fruit Coolers *Agua Fresca*

Cooling Mexican fruit drinks are just right for a really hot summer day. Fruits are very much a part of Mexican cooking. Try this basic recipe and then experiment with different fruits to come up with your own refreshing combination of flavors.

Makes 12 cups

Ingredients

fresh strawberries, cantaloupe, raspberries, pineapple, or mangoes, or a combination of these (totaling 3 cups chopped)
8 cups cold water

¾ cup sugar
ice cubes
extra fruit for serving

On your mark, get set, blend!

- Wash the fruit. Cut the fruit into chunks and measure 3 cups.
- Ask your adult assistant to help with the next step.
- Place the fruit in the jar of a blender and add 1 cup of the water. Press the lid firmly in place. Blend at high speed until smooth.
- Pour the blended fruit liquid into a strainer and strain over a large bowl. Using a wooden spoon, stir and press down on the fruit to extract all the liquid. Discard the fruit pulp.
- Once the liquid is strained, add the sugar, remaining 7 cups water, and ice cubes to the large bowl.
- Stir well to combine the ingredients and dissolve the sugar.
- Serve cold in tall glasses with extra chunks of fruit.

Mexican Hot Chocolate *Chocolate a la Mexicana*

Chocolate comes from the seeds of the cacao plant. The ancient Aztec and Maya peoples believed that this dark, luscious creation was almost supernatural, so they called it the "food of the gods." It gave them energy and lightened their spirits. No exploration of Mexican cooking would be complete without a chocolate recipe. Here is a simple and easy way to prepare the world's favorite hot drink. As you enjoy it, remember that we owe this heavenly ingredient to Mexico.

Makes 6 cups

Ingredients

3 round tablets sweetened Mexican chocolate
6 cups whole milk
1 tablespoon masa harina (optional)

On your mark, get set, cook!

- Place all the ingredients in a 3-quart saucepan.
- Cook on medium heat until the chocolate melts, stirring occasionally to make sure the mixture is smooth.
- Bring to a boil; this will take 10 to 12 minutes. Be careful it does not boil over.
- Remove from the heat. Beat with a whisk or electric hand mixer until the mixture is thick and foamy. Pour into individual mugs and serve hot.

ALL ABOUT CHILE PEPPERS

Christopher Columbus made a mistake. In searching for that most desirable of spices, black pepper, he thought he had found it when he first tasted chiles. Chiles were spicy and hot, so he referred to them as "chilli peppers." Even though he was not completely correct, the name stuck and the rest, as they say, is history.

Chiles have been a part of the Mexican kitchen for thousands of years. They add flavor and excitement to any recipe they season. Did you know that chiles are a fruit from a group of plants called capsicum and that there are over one hundred varieties? These colorful fruits range widely in type, size, shape, and heat. They're packed with vitamins A and C. Hot or mild, chile peppers are really very cool once you get to know them.

Many people incorrectly believe that all chiles are hot, so they won't even give them a try. As a result, these healthy fruits are very misunderstood. *"That will taste too hot!"* How many times have you said that to yourself when you've seen a dish on a menu that has chile peppers in it? But the fact is that some are quite mild tasting.

There are a few important things to know before you begin to cook with chiles. Any experienced cook will tell you that some precautions are essential to make sure your cooking experience is a pleasant one. If you follow these simple guidelines, you'll get the best results and give your dishes an authentic Mexican flavor.

HOW TO HANDLE CHILES

Wear rubber or disposable latex kitchen gloves as a precaution to keep your skin from contacting the hot oils in the pepper, called capsaicin, which can stay on unprotected skin for several hours. Remember, never touch your eyes, nose, or any other part of your face or skin when working with hot peppers, to avoid passing on the capsaicin. Rinse your gloves and dry them with paper towels before removing them, and then give your hands a thorough washing with hot soapy water.

HOW TO PREPARE CHILES FOR RECIPES

Rule # 1: Slip on your rubber or latex gloves before beginning.

Preparing Fresh Chiles: *Rinse the chile in cold water, never hot. Break off the stem, pull it away from the chile, and discard. To open the chile, lay it on a cutting board and slice it lengthwise with the tip of a sharp knife. Once it is open, you will notice the seeds and the lighter-colored veins inside. These contain most of the heat. If you are like most people and don't want your dish to be too hot, remove the seeds under cold running water. If you like your recipe spicy, leave all or some of them.*

Preparing Dried Chiles (Method #1): *If the dried chile is very dusty, rinse it in cold water and pat dry with a paper towel. Place the dried chile in a small bowl and add 1 cup of hot water. In 20 to 30 minutes, the chile skin will soften and puff up slightly, looking more like it did when it was fresh. Remove the stem and seeds and follow the directions in your recipe. Save the soaking water to use for an extra-flavorful liquid in your recipes.*

Preparing Dried Chiles (Method #2): *Heat a dry heavy-bottomed or cast-iron frying pan on medium-low heat for 3 to 4 minutes. Place the chile in the pan and cover it with a small metal lid to flatten it. Toast the chile for 1 to 2 minutes on each side, or until the skin begins to soften and change color. Remove to a bowl and follow the directions above to soak the chile.*

TYPES OF FRESH HOT CHILES

Jalapeño: *The jalapeño is probably the most familiar of all Mexican peppers. This famous rich green hot pepper can be found in salsas and sauces, stuffed with cream cheese, on a plate of nachos, spicing up a jar of pepper jam, or topping tacos. The jalapeño, which generally measures about 2 1/2 inches long and 3/4 inch wide, originated in Mexico. Available fresh or canned, it ranges from hot to very hot. You should not handle a jalapeño without gloves. Remove the veins and seeds from the inside before using it in your recipe.*

Serrano: *The serrano pepper is very popular in Mexico. It is smaller in size than a jalapeño and has a bullet shape. It is packed with heat and flavor; use it with caution.*

TYPES OF DRIED CHILES

Ancho: *The ancho is reddish brown in color when dried and changes to a brick red when soaked in water. It is four to five inches long and packed with smoky flavor. The ancho is probably the most common dried pepper used in the cooking of Mexico. When fresh, it is called poblano and is dark green in color. The ancho can be soaked and ground for many different recipes. The heat ranges from mild to medium-hot.*

Chipotle: *A chipotle is a jalapeño pepper that is dried and smoked. You can buy chipotles canned and packed in vinegar or in a sweet red sauce called adobo. You can also buy them dried. The smoking process fills the chile with a great deep flavor.*

Pasilla: *The pasilla is wrinkled, long and narrow, and raisin brown in color. In fact, in Spanish its name means "little raisin." Pasilla chiles are mild to medium-hot. They are best used in recipes for sauces and with seafood.*

CHILE WISDOM

You ate a chile that was just too hot and now your mouth is on fire?
Drink a glass of milk or have some yogurt or another dairy product. Try eating a piece of bread or tortilla. Do not drink water, as it will only make your problem worse.

You forgot to wear gloves and now your hands are starting to burn?
Soak your hands in cold salted water. Or add a tablespoon of bleach to a large bowl of cold water and soak until the burning fades. If all else fails, rub a little toothpaste on your skin.

You don't know how many chiles to use?
If you don't like a lot of heat, start with fewer chiles than the recipe calls for. It is easy to add heat to a recipe, but very difficult to take it away. If you find the dish just too hot after you've made it, you can cool it down by adding more tomatoes, rice, or potatoes, or by topping the dish with more cheese and sour cream.

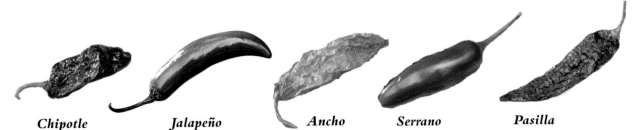

Chipotle   **Jalapeño**   **Ancho**   **Serrano**   **Pasilla**

Helpful Kitchen Equipment and Utensils

CUTTING BOARD

SAUCEPANS WITH LIDS

LARGE METAL SLOTTED SPOON

BAKING PAN

ASSORTED KNIVES

STOCKPOT WITH LID

SPATULA

BLENDER

ELECTRIC HAND MIXER

SKILLETS (FRYING PANS)

CAST-IRON SKILLET (FRYING PAN)

WHISK

MIXING BOWL

BAKING SHEET

CHEESE GRATER

METAL COLANDER

TONGS

STRAINER

RUBBER OR LATEX KITCHEN GLOVES

DEEP-FRY THERMOMETER

VEGETABLE BRUSH

WIRE COOLING RACK

ROUND POTATO MASHER

POTATO PEELER

ESSENTIAL INGREDIENTS IN THE MEXICAN KITCHEN

ALLSPICE
These dried berries are from Jamaica and are available whole or ground. If you have a spice grinder, it is recommended that you buy them whole and grind them yourself for maximum flavor.

AVOCADOS
Avocados are a fruit full of surprises. They are packed with protein and natural oils, and they have been cultivated for over seven thousand years. If they are not ripe when you buy them, they will ripen in a few days if kept out of the sun. You know an avocado is ripe when you gently squeeze it and it is just a little soft, like a tennis ball. When ripe, the fruit's flavor is best described as "buttery." For the recipes in this book, look for the Hass variety. Hass avocados are small and have a dark, slightly bumpy outer skin. To prevent the chopped avocado from turning brown, place the pit in the bowl with the chopped fruit and cover with plastic wrap.

CHILES
Read all about fresh and dried chiles on page 72.

CILANTRO
Cilantro is an herb also known as fresh coriander or Chinese parsley. It adds great flavor to Mexican dishes. Cilantro looks almost identical to parsley and is easily confused with it, but it has a bolder flavor and a spicy aroma. It should be washed to remove any sand still clinging to the stems or leaves. Wrapped in plastic, it will keep for about a week in the refrigerator.

DRIED BEANS
Beans are one of the most common ingredients in Mexican cooking. Dried red pinto beans are very common in northern Mexico and black beans are more common in the south. Both varieties will work for the recipes in this book. Rinse beans in a colander and then pour them onto a tray in a single layer. Carefully check for and remove any tiny stones or shriveled, very dark beans.

GARLIC
Garlic is a member of the onion family and a valuable flavor maker in Mexican cooking. When you purchase garlic, look for large bulbs that are hard and solid. Inside the bulb are cloves. To use the cloves, first separate them from the bulb. With the flat side of a knife, give them a good whack, then remove the white paperlike skin and cut off the dark tip. The cloves can be chopped into small pieces, mashed, or cut into thin slices. Many nutritionists believe that garlic has great health benefits because it is rich in minerals. The world is separated into two groups of people—those who love garlic and those who don't. Which are you?

LARD

Lard is pork fat that is cooked down into a solid by a process called rendering. Many people are reluctant to use lard because they believe that it is very high in cholesterol and fat. Actually, according to the USDA, lard has only half the cholesterol and two-thirds the saturated fat of butter. Today the modern Mexican cook uses lard in moderation, and you should, too. Consider buying lard only if you are able to find it fresh from a Mexican grocer, because commercially produced lard is made with hydrogenated oils and is not recommended. Vegetable, canola, and corn oil are excellent substitutes.

MASA HARINA

Masa harina is a specially ground cornmeal and is the basic ingredient in tortillas. It is generally available in the baking section of your local supermarket. Quick-cooking grits are an excellent substitute. Once the package is opened, place the masa harina in an airtight container and it will keep for up to a year.

MEXICAN CHOCOLATE

The chocolate of Mexico comes in different sizes and shapes. Harder and coarser than other chocolates, it is sweetened and flavored with cinnamon and sometimes ground nuts. The most common packaging is a box of six 3-ounce tablets or disks, which are perforated into pie-shaped wedges. Mexican chocolate is available in supermarkets or specialty food stores.

QUESO FRESCO

Queso fresco means "fresh cheese." It is an important element in Mexican cooking because of its subtle flavor. Queso fresco is available in Mexican markets or specialty cheese stores. Keep it refrigerated and well wrapped. It should be used within three to five days of purchase.

TOMATILLOS

Tomatillos are a small, green, tart-tasting fruit. They are often confused with green tomatoes. The papery outer husk needs to be peeled away and removed before using, and then the fruit should be washed to remove any sticky residue. Look for firm, solid tomatillos that fill the skin completely. They will keep in the refrigerator for several weeks.

TORTILLAS

Mexican tortillas usually contain just corn flour (called masa) and water. Tortillas made with wheat flour are also popular, especially in northern Mexico. Tortillas may be available in supermarkets or specialty food stores. Look for ones that are made without chemical preservatives or added fats. If you have a Mexican specialty store near you, chances are you will find excellent tortillas. Keep them well wrapped and refrigerated for up to a week after purchase. They also freeze very well. Thaw frozen tortillas before attempting to separate them.

INDEX

METRIC CONVERSION CHART

You can use the chart below to convert from U.S. measurements to the metric system.

Weight
1 ounce = 28 grams
1/2 pound (8 ounces) = 227 grams
1 pound = .45 kilogram
2.2 pounds = 1 kilogram

Liquid volume
1 teaspoon = 5 milliliters
1 tablespoon = 15 milliliters
1 fluid ounce = 30 milliliters
1 cup = 240 milliliters (.24 liter)
1 pint = 480 milliliters (.48 liter)
1 quart = .95 liter

Length
1/4 inch = .6 centimeter
1/2 inch = 1.25 centimeters
1 inch = 2.5 centimeters

Temperature
100°F = 40°C
110°F = 45°C
212°F = 100°C (boiling point of water)
350°F = 180°C
375°F = 190°C
400°F = 200°C
425°F = 220°C
450°F = 235°C
(To convert temperatures in Fahrenheit to Celsius, subtract 32 and multiply by .56)